Go-Go Boy Bobby

by Sam Morrison
illustrations by Robert Hedges

Go-Go Boy Bobby

By Sam Morrison

All Copyright © 2023 by Sam Morrison

Publishing all rights reserved worldwide. All rights reserved as sole property of the Author. The Author guarantees all content is original and does not infringe upon the legal rights of any other person or work.

No part of this book may be reproduced, stored in a retrieval system, or transmitted in any form or by any means, without expressed written permission of the author.

Published by: GWN Publishing, LLC
www.gwnpublishing.com

Illustrations by: Robert Hedges
Production Design: Kristina Conatser
www.capturedbykcdesigns.com

Paperback ISBN: 978-1-959608-49-3
E-Book ISBN: 978-1-959608-48-6
Hardcover ISBN: 978-1-959608-50-9

Dedication

To Tim, who always brings me back to reality.
And my children who fill me with love.

Go-Go Boy Bobby

by Sam Morrison
illustrations by Robert Hedges

Go-go boy Bobby, he is always on the run.

He is so busy, he has so much fun!

He runs around, like he
has a motor inside.

He moves so fast, there
is no time to hide.

He jumps into the pool and swims just like a fish.

He wanted to be fast, and it looks like he got his wish!

While racing down the field,
he kicks a soccer ball.

Bobby is careful not to trip.
He doesn't want to fall.

He likes to race while walking his dog.

He runs so fast he jumps over logs!

He tries to see how
fast he can go,

putting on the
stopwatch and providing
quite a show!

He likes to have contests
with other people too,

in order to show others
what he can do!

He gets into his special racing stance,

with a concentrated face and a serious glance.

Someone counts down
from three to one.

Then someone shouts go!
And the race has begun!

Bobby takes off, without looking back,

To see how he smoked the others on the track!

When he makes it to the finish line,

go-go boy Bobby is feeling fine!

So, when you see someone
with energy to burn,

Just ask them to race and
it will be your turn,

To see them explode with
energy so pure,

That they will be good
friends for sure!

Why is it that Bobby needs to go-go-go?

With all his energy, I am surprised he doesn't glow!

Movement helps us to learn and explore,

And when we have the energy, this does not feel like a chore!

So energy, when burned the right way,

Can help you to think, become strong and learn to play.

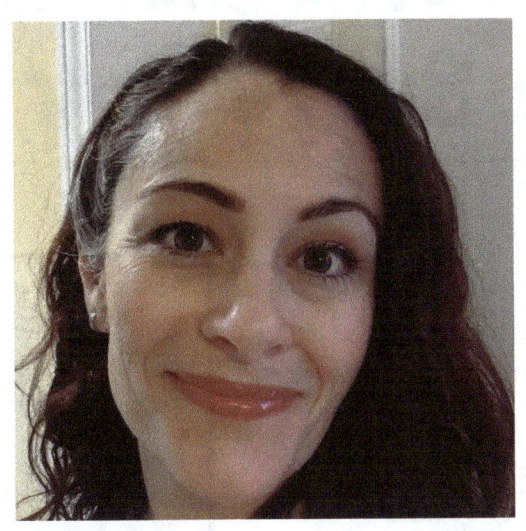

About The Author

Sam Morrison is a wife and mother of three sons. She works in the medical field. Sam loves art, literature, hiking and a passion for animals.

Look for other Books in the Bobby Boy Series

Find Grumpy Boy Bobby on Amazon and anywhere books are sold. Scan the QR code below to order your copy.

Coming soon!

Generous Boy Bobby

Printed in the USA
CPSIA information can be obtained
at www.ICGtesting.com
LVHW050727221023
761786LV00006B/56